21st
Century
Skills Library

COOL CAREERS

ELECTRICIAN

MICHAEL TEITELBAUM

Published in the United States of America by
Cherry Lake Publishing, Ann Arbor, Michigan
www.cherrylakepublishing.com

Content Adviser
Paul Rosenberg

Credits
Photos: Cover and page 1, ©iStockphoto.com/lisafx; page 4, ©iStockphoto.com/
wynnter; page 7, ©Shane White/Shutterstock, Inc.; page 8, ©iStockphoto.com/
briannolan; page 10, ©Enruta/Dreamstime.com; page 12, ©Monkeybusinessimages/
Dreamstime.com; page 17, ©Bill Bachmann/Alamy; page 18, ©Lisa F. Young/
Shutterstock, Inc.; page 20, ©Juice Images/Alamy; page 23, ©Razvanjp/Dreamstime.
com; page 24, ©Gary718/Dreamstime.com; page 27, ©Lisafx/Dreamstime.com;
page 28, ©Monkey Business Images/Shutterstock, Inc.

Library of Congress Cataloging-in-Publication Data
Teitelbaum, Michael.
  Electrician/by Michael Teitelbaum.
    p. cm.—(Cool careers)
  Includes bibliographical references and index.
  ISBN-13: 978-1-60279-936-3 (lib. bdg.)
  ISBN-10: 1-60279-936-9 (lib. bdg.)
  1. Electrical engineering—Vocational guidance—Juvenile literature.
  2. Electricians—Juvenile literature. I. Title. II. Series.
   TK159.T45 2010
   621.3023—dc22   2010000686

Cherry Lake Publishing would like to acknowledge
the work of The Partnership for 21st Century Skills.
Please visit *www.21stcenturyskills.org* for more information.

Printed in the United States of America
Corporate Graphics Inc.
July 2010
CLFA07

COOL CAREERS

ELECTRICIAN

TABLE OF CONTENTS

CHAPTER ONE
A POWER-FULL IDEA

Imagine a world of darkness. A place where light comes only from fire and the sun. What kind of world

Benjamin Franklin invented the lightning rod.

would that be? Actually, it's the world that people lived in for most of human history. It's the world before humans made use of electricity.

Electricity has only been used during the past 100 to 150 years. Think of how important electricity has become in that time. We would not be able to light our homes and businesses without it. We also need it to power the electronics we use every day. Computers, TVs, and air conditioners run on electricity. So do machines in hospitals. Don't forget about equipment in factories. You can probably think of many more things that would not work without electricity.

In June 1752, Benjamin Franklin flew a kite during a lightning storm. He hung a metal key from the kite's string. Electricity traveled down the string when the kite was struck by lightning. This caused the key to spark. Franklin discovered that lightning was caused by electricity. He also realized that electricity could travel along power lines.

One hundred years passed before scientists discovered how to turn electricity into light. Many scientists around the world helped with the invention of the lightbulb. Some included Joseph Swan in England and Thomas Edison in the United States.

Edison's idea for the lightbulb was a part of a larger plan. He invented a system that would create electricity. It would also deliver it to homes and businesses. People began using this system in the late 1880s. Since then, electricians have had the job of setting up that system. They must also maintain it.

Electricity travels along a path from where it is produced to where it is used. Electricians make sure the electricity moves safely at each step along that path.

LEARNING & INNOVATION SKILLS

Many people helped develop the lightbulb. The person most people remember is Thomas Edison. Edison wanted to bring light to homes, businesses, and streets. His thinking went beyond lightbulbs. He had the big picture in mind. He knew a system was needed to deliver electricity. Can you think of other inventors who kept the big picture in mind when creating their inventions?

Some electricians work at the power plants where electricity is produced. Others work on power lines. These lines carry electricity from power plants to homes

Electricians can't let a fear of heights get in the way of doing their job!

and businesses. Some electricians work on the wires, outlets, and switches inside buildings.

Houses often lose electricity when power lines are knocked down during big storms. Electricians hurry to the scene. They fix the power lines and bring power back to buildings left in the dark. These electricians must often work outside during storms. They face the elements, such as wind,

Electricians know how serious a blackout can be. They work very hard to repair downed power lines.

rain, and snow. They work under dangerous conditions. Electricity and water are a deadly mix!

Electricians install wires and panels in new buildings. They read **blueprints** to see where everything goes. Electricians are also called in to repair wiring in older buildings. Old wiring can cause fires. Electricians may replace the panels, wiring, and outlets in these older buildings. This makes the electrical system work more effectively and safely. As keepers of the power system, electricians have many jobs!

LIFE & CAREER SKILLS

People in some jobs perform the same duties in the same place every day. An electrician's work is different. Projects can vary from one job site to the next. So can working conditions. Electricians must be able to adapt to different situations and still do their jobs well. One project might take place in a small basement. The next might take place in a more open area. No two jobs are exactly the same. For many, this variety is an advantage that attracted them to the career. Can you think of some pros and cons of having a job in which roles and conditions often change?

CHAPTER TWO
ON THE JOB

It all begins at the power plant. Big machines called **generators** change forms of energy into electricity. The energy might come from burning fuels. These include coal,

Electricians must be very careful when working with transformers and other electrical equipment.

oil, or gas. These fuels produce harmful waste that is released into the air.

There are also cleaner ways to generate the energy needed to create electricity. **Hydropower** uses the force of rushing water to power the generators. Wind power uses the force of wind. Solar power comes from sunlight.

Electricians take care of the equipment at the power plants. They make sure the power keeps moving.

Electricians who work in power plants are called powerhouse electricians. They set up and maintain the power plant's equipment. They connect large cables from generators to **transformers**. Transformers can increase or decrease the **voltage** of electricity. Voltage is the force that pushes electricity through electric power lines.

Transformers at power plants are called step-up transformers. They increase voltage. This allows the electricity to travel longer distances while using less energy. This electricity is dangerous and not ready for people to use.

The electricity travels out of the power plant through power lines. Some power lines run under the ground. Others run above ground. They are attached to large metal towers and wooden or concrete utility poles.

Electricians who work on power lines are called lineworkers. They put up new power lines. These connect the power plant and the buildings where people live and work.

Once the lines are up, the lineworkers keep them running properly. They also fix the lines when they are damaged.

Lineworkers use special equipment and clothing to help them stay safe. One tool they use is a truck that has a bucket on the back. The bucket is big enough for a lineworker to stand in. A long arm raises the bucket. That way, the worker can reach the tops of utility poles and towers. The bucket is

How many outlets are in your home?
An electrician set all of them up!

made of **insulated** material. This means the material does not allow electricity to pass through. The bucket keeps the worker safe from powerful electricity. Lineworkers also protect themselves by wearing special gloves and boots.

Of all electricians, lineworkers have the most dangerous job. They must repair power lines no matter the situation. This often means working in the dark. Rain, snow, and high winds can't stop a lineworker, either. The power must be restored.

Electricity travels along power lines from the power plant to a **substation**. There, it runs through a step-down transformer. This transformer lowers the electricity's voltage for the final part of its trip. The electricity then travels into neighborhoods through feeder lines. These lines spread out from the substation.

A distribution transformer lowers the voltage enough to make the electricity safe and useful for homes and businesses. Lineworkers maintain step-down transformers and substations. They also maintain feeder lines and distribution transformers.

A lower-voltage power line carries the electricity from the distribution transformer into a building. That's where the inside electrician takes over.

There are two types of inside electricians: construction electricians and maintenance electricians. Construction electricians set up the electrical systems in new buildings.

Maintenance electricians repair or replace existing electrical systems. They also repair electrical equipment.

Construction electricians begin with blueprints. These are drawings that show where to put wires, outlets, and other electrical equipment in a building.

A construction electrician arrives after the house is framed out. The wooden or metal framework of a building is in place. But there are no finished walls yet. This makes it easier for the electrician to run wires through the building.

The first step in wiring a new building is to run cables inside the walls. This creates paths to every section of the building. The cables contain the wires that electricity will travel through. Next, boxes that will hold outlets and light switches are attached to the walls.

The construction electrician runs the main electrical line into a service panel inside the house. A service panel is a box that holds the circuit breakers. Circuit breakers are switches that flip if there is a problem with the electricity. Power stops flowing when a breaker flips. An electrician can then fix the problem before flipping the breaker back on.

One main line comes into the service panel. The electrician creates many smaller lines leading out of the panel. Each line has its own breaker. It goes to a different section of the building. The service panel also has a main breaker that can shut down the power to the whole building.

What happens when the wiring, breakers, and boxes are in place? That is when electricians install lights, switches, and outlets. Sometimes they add wires for telephones and other devices. Wires for heating and cooling systems might also be installed.

Maintenance electricians work on completed buildings. Their jobs can vary. They repair or replace electric systems and electronic machines. They might even rewire an entire house.

Older houses sometimes have out-of-date fuse boxes. Electricians often replace them with more modern circuit breakers. Sometimes, homeowners will hire electricians to install things such as ceiling fans.

LEARNING & INNOVATION SKILLS

Imagine that you are planning to build a new house. You meet with an architect and an electrician. They suggest regular ways of lighting, heating, and cooling your new home. But you would like to make use of solar, wind, and **geothermal** energy. How would you convince them that this would be better for the environment?

Some maintenance electricians work in factories. They fix motors. They even fix robots that are used to do assembly jobs. They also examine electrical equipment to make sure everything is working. This helps them find problems before they become big issues.

Electricians use many different tools. Some include hand tools such as wire strippers and screwdrivers. They also use power tools such as drills. These are common tools that are also used by other kinds of construction workers.

Electricians also use special tools that other workers do not. Circuit testers check whether or not electricity is flowing correctly. Voltmeters and other instruments measure the amount of electricity running through a system. These tools help electricians make sure connections are set up correctly and safely.

Lineworkers often use big machinery. They use cranes. Cranes help them put utility poles into place. Sometimes powerhouse electricians use remote-controlled robots. These help with dangerous tasks involving high voltage.

Some electricians repair and maintain large, complex pieces of equipment.

CHAPTER THREE
WHAT IT TAKES

W
hat does it take to become an electrician?
Electricians need clear and focused minds. They must pay

Time in the classroom is
part of the training process
for future electricians.

careful attention to their work. Otherwise, they can put themselves and others in danger.

Electricians need to be strong. They have to be able to lift heavy items. How heavy? They might have to lift more than 50 pounds (23 kilograms). They also have to be able to bend metal **conduit** pipes. **Stamina** is also important. Electricians may need to climb up tall poles. They may have to stay balanced there for a long time during bad weather. They might also have to stand or kneel for hours. At the same time, they must stay focused on the tiniest details of their work.

Electricians need to be at least 18 years old. A high school education is very important. Classes in shop, physics, drafting, and math are recommended.

Most electricians start out as **apprentices**. They work with experienced electricians. This kind of practice is the best way to learn the skills they need.

Apprentices work during the day. They get paid while learning the job. At night, they take classes to learn about how electricity works. They learn how to read blueprints. They learn the rules of safe wiring. They also take classes in math, electronics, and job safety.

You must take a test before you can become an apprentice. The test measures math, reading, and motor skills. People who pass the test have to wait for an apprenticeship to open up. This could take months or longer.

Apprentices begin with simple tasks. These include drilling holes or attaching conduit pipes. They move on to more difficult tasks as they gain skills. Apprentices train on the job for 3 to 5 years.

Many electricians keep taking classes after they finish their apprenticeships. They learn about telephones, computers, and other topics. An electrician's next step is to take a licensing exam. A license proves that the electrician has worked hard and put in years of study and training. Electricians continue

Experienced electricians supervise the work of apprentices.

learning and training even after getting licensed. They need to keep up with new technology. They also learn about changes in the field.

LIFE & CAREER SKILLS

Learning the basics of being an electrician can help you adapt to roles in other fields. There are many careers that someone with training as an electrician can consider. You might get a job installing or repairing heating or air conditioning units. You could specialize in setting up home entertainment equipment. You might find that you enjoy setting up and repairing elevators. The list goes on!

Mike Eads is a maintenance electrician at Cornell Medical College in New York City. Mike started out as an apprentice. "I began working with a licensed construction electrician," he recalls. "At first he had me go get tools and parts. Then I started drilling holes and mounting boxes. In time, I began pulling cables and twisting wires together." Learning by doing a task on the job is important, he explains. As he learned more, he was allowed to do more. "Slowly, I built up my knowledge."

Eads studied in school for 6 months. He learned about how electricity works and other topics. Eventually, he became licensed and started his own business. What does he like best about being an electrician? The job, he says, is "always interesting because there are always new things to learn." Most electricians would agree.

LEARNING & INNOVATION SKILLS

You probably know that electricians must have expert knowledge of electrical equipment. But did you know that they should also be good team players? Being a strong member of the team means always doing careful work. It also means cooperating. The ability to work effectively with others is very important. The idea goes beyond just working well with other electricians. Electricians may interact with other members of a construction team. This could include architects and interior designers. An electrician may also have contact with clients. For that reason, having strong customer service skills also comes in handy.

Do you work well with others? Electricians must often work as a team to get the job done.

CHAPTER FOUR
A BRIGHT FUTURE

J ob opportunities for electricians are expected
to grow. More electricians will be needed as the population

*Electricians have to keep up
with new ways to power cities.*

grows. They'll set up and maintain more electrical equipment and wiring.

Demand for electricity continues to rise. This means electric companies will need to build more power plants. This will create new jobs for electricians. Demand for expert electricians will also increase as new technology appears. Buildings of the future will need wiring for more advanced computers. The same will be true for more advanced communications equipment. Electricians with knowledge of voice, data, and video electronics will be in greater demand.

Factories continue to add robots and advanced manufacturing systems. These will require the setup and maintenance of detailed wiring systems.

The nation's **infrastructure** always needs to be maintained and upgraded to meet new safety codes. Utility poles, power lines, and other parts need to be fixed or replaced as they age.

Lighting and heating systems continue to become more advanced. Modern buildings often have lighting and heating that is controlled by computers. The electricians of the future will need to know how to work on these systems.

The search for clean energy continues. Experts try to provide electricity for more people without damaging the environment. Advances in wind and solar power will become more important. Electricians will have to be trained in these areas as they develop.

Electrician Mike Eads remains positive about the future for those interested in becoming electricians. He is seeing more advanced electrical setups. Smart houses are one example. In a smart house, he explains, "the electrical systems are linked to a computer system." Some of these systems, he notes, can be controlled over the Internet.

21ST CENTURY CONTENT

The United States Department of Labor projects that the employment rate for electricians will grow by 12 percent between 2008 and 2018. This makes the possibility of a career as an electrician a positive one. This is true even during difficult economic times. The outlook is good for electricians.

Why do you think electricians are in demand even during tough financial periods? Hint: Think about how electricians help us. Do people always need their services?

Wind and solar power are promising sources of energy. But as Eads points out, "our electrical infrastructure will have to be remade to make the most of these. The electricians of the future will be doing that work."

Have you ever seen solar panels on the roof of a building?

Picture a normal day in your life. Now imagine that same day without electricity. How would it be different? By now, you probably realize that electricity plays an important role in many parts of our lives. Products that use electricity help us in many ways. They allow us to see in the dark. They allow us to heat our homes. Electricity also powers the machines that entertain us. Someone will always be needed to create and maintain power systems. Will that someone be you?

Think about how the work of electricians affects our lives the next time you flip a switch or watch television!

SOME WELL-KNOWN PEOPLE IN THE WORLD OF ELECTRICITY

Thomas Alva Edison (1847–1931) was a key figure in bringing electricity into people's homes and businesses. This great inventor also created the movie camera. He is credited with inventing the lightbulb. Others, however, helped with that invention. In 1880, Edison patented a system for distributing electricity. Two years later, he switched on the country's first electrical generating station and power distribution system. This system brought electricity to 59 people in New York City. Within a few years, power stations and distribution lines started springing up around the world.

Benjamin Franklin (1706–1790) was a Founding Father of the United States. This talented man was an author, printer, and politician. He was also a soldier, scientist, and inventor. His famous kite experiment proved that lightning contained electricity. Franklin also invented the lightning rod. He coined many terms we now use when we talk about electricity. *Battery*, *conductor*, and *charge* are some examples. So are *electric shock* and *electrician*.

Nikola Tesla (1856–1943) experimented with electricity around the same time as Edison. In 1880, Tesla discovered a new way to produce electricity. It involved using a rotating magnetic field. This was more efficient than Edison's way. By the 1890s, Tesla's alternating current was providing electricity to approximately 80 percent of U.S. households. It is now used around the world. His invention of the Tesla coil in 1891 made wireless radios possible. The coil is still used in many radios and television sets. He also proved that Earth itself could be used as an electrical conductor.

GLOSSARY

apprentices (uh-PREN-tiss-iz) people who learn a trade by working with an expert

blueprints (BLOO-printss) drawings or plans for a project

conduit (KON-doo-it) pipe that protects electric wires

generators (JEN-uh-ray-turz) machines that produce electricity

geothermal (jee-oh-THUR-muhl) having to do with the heat inside the earth and its use

hydropower (hye-droh-POU-ur) electricity created by the movement of water

infrastructure (IN-fruh-struk-chur) the basic framework of a system

insulated (IN-suh-lay-tid) treated in a special way to keep electricity from passing through

stamina (STAM-uh-nuh) the ability to continue doing something for a long period of time

substation (SUB-stay-shuhn) a system of structures that, among other functions, changes the force of electricity from one level to another

transformers (transs-FORM-urz) devices that raise or lower the force of electricity

voltage (VOHL-tij) a measure of the force of electricity

FOR MORE INFORMATION

BOOKS

Lockwood, Sophie. *Super Cool Science Experiments: Electricity.* Ann Arbor, MI: Cherry Lake Publishing, 2010.

Newell, Ella. *Turn on the Light: How Electricity Works.* Vero Beach, FL: Rourke Publishing, 2008.

Venezia, Mike. *Thomas Edison: Inventor with a Lot of Bright Ideas.* New York: Children's Press, 2009.

WEB SITES

Bureau of Labor Statistics—Electrician
www.bls.gov/k12/build06.htm
Learn more about what electricians do.

EIA Energy Kids—Electricity
tonto.eia.doe.gov/kids/energy.cfm?page=electricity_home-basics
Find out more about electricity at this site from the U.S. Energy Information Administration.

Hampshire Fire and Rescue Service—Electricity
www.hantsfire.gov.uk/electricity
Find more information about electricity and how it works.

INDEX

ABOUT THE AUTHOR

Michael Teitelbaum has been a writer and editor of children's books and magazines for more than 20 years. He is the author of *Jackie Robinson: Champion for Equality*, published by Sterling Publishing, and *The Scary States of America*, published by Delacorte. Michael and his wife, Sheleigah, split their time between New York City and their 170-year-old farmhouse in the Catskill Mountains of upstate New York.